Candle Making
made easy

Candle Making
made easy

Series Editors: Susan & Martin Penny

David & Charles

A DAVID & CHARLES BOOK

First published in the UK in 1999

A catalogue record for this book is available from the British Library.

ISBN 0 7153 0975 7

Series Editors: Susan & Martin Penny
Designed and produced by Penny & Penny
Illustrations: Fred Fieber at Red Crayola
Photography: Jon Stone

Printed in Italy by LEGO S.p.A. Vicenza
for David & Charles
Brunel House Newton Abbot Devon

Contents

Introduction to Candle Making

Candle Making Made Easy is a complete guide to the craft of candle making; read on for useful advice on choosing the correct wax and wick; help with finding the right equipment; and guidance on accident prevention and fire precautions to help you make a variety of moulded, rolled, dipped and decorated candles safely at home

Essential equipment

Below is a list of equipment needed for candle making:

- **Double boiler** – will prevent the wax from overheating. Fill the bottom with water. and put paraffin wax in the top; or use a saucepan with a trivet or rack in the bottom and a metal jug, bowl or tin can on top.
- **Saucepan** – used for heating wax above 100°C (212°F).
- **Dipping can** – a metal container tall enough to take the height of the finished candle and narrow enough not to use too much wax.
- **Egg Poacher** – for melting small quantities of wax.
- **Heat source** – gas or electric ring.
- **Pouring jug** – metal jug for filling moulds.
- **Water bath** – needs to be deep enough for the water to come up to the top of the wax in the mould; and if using a flexible mould, no more than 5cm (2in) larger.
- **Wicking needle** – steel needle, knitting needle, skewer or a large eyed sewing needle for securing wicks and making holes in flexible moulds.
- **Thermometer** – a cooking thermometer.
- **Scales** – kitchen scales for weighing wax and stearin.
- **Mould seal** – putty like compound for sealing the mould to prevent leakage.
- **Hairdryer** – for softening moulding wax.
- **Craft knife** – for cutting beeswax sheets.

Which wax ?

- **Paraffin wax** – manufactured as blocks or pellets; pure or with 10% stearin added.

- **Beeswax** – a natural wax which is added to candle wax to increase burning time. Also produced as flat sheets for rolled candles.
- **Microcrystalline hard or soft wax** – an opaque wax that is the main ingredient of modelling wax.
- **Overdipping wax** – gives a tough, high gloss finish to paraffin wax candle.
- **Dip and carve wax** – can be moulded at low temperatures.

Additives

Additives are used to enhance the performance and appearance of candles.

- **Stearin** – additive used in rigid moulded candles, to aid release from the mould.
- **Vybar** – use in rubber moulds in place of stearin which will chemically rot them.
- **Dye** – use dye discs or powdered colour.
- **Perfume** – candle scent added to hot wax.

Which wick?

✔ Most candles need a square braided wick, graded according to the size of the candle

✔ Beeswax candles need a round braided wick, twice the width of ordinary candles

✔ Votives need a wire or paper-cored wick held in place by a wick sustainer

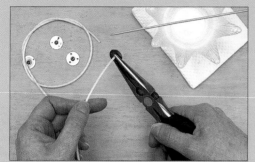

✔ Use a special wick for floating candles

Tips for making candles

✔ Cover your working area with newspaper as coloured wax can discolour some surfaces

✔ Use clean and dry, cardboard waxed milk, juice or yogurt cartons as moulds

✔ Trays of plastic sweet moulds make good floating candle moulds

✔ Small amounts of left-over wax can be saved and re-used for making candles

✔ After making, leave the candle for at least 24 hours before burning

✔ Always use the correct wick: too thick and the candle will soot and smoke; too thin and it will not burn properly

✔ Make sure the wick is straight and in the middle of the candle

✔ Trim the wick to 1-2cm (¹/₂-³/₄in) so that it burns without smoking

✔ Rub the outside of a rubber mould with washing-up liquid to remove the candle

✔ Always use an unprimed wick with a rubber mould to limit the size of the hole

Common sense with wax

Molten wax can be a very dangerous substance if handled incorrectly. It is important that you are aware of the potential problems and know how to deal with them safely should they happen.

Melting Wax

● The safest way to melt wax is in a double boiler, but wax melted in this way will only reach the temperature of the water, 100°C (212°F). This temperature is high enough for most candles.

● If the wax needs to be hotter, use an open saucepan, which is a less safe method of heating wax. Heat the wax slowly, monitoring the temperature with a thermometer. Do not leave the pan unattended as the wax can ignite if it gets too hot.

Fire!

● At temperatures below 100°C (212°F) wax is unlikely to ignite. If heated to a higher temperature, wax should be treated like hot cooking oil, which is highly flammable.

● If the wax does catch fire switch off the heat immediately and cover the pan with a damp cloth or the saucepan lid. Leave until the pan has gone cold before removing the cover or moving the saucepan.

● Do not try to put the fire out with water.

Accident Prevention

● Turn the pan handles inward on the cooker.

● Do not pour melted wax down the drain.

● Don't guess: use a thermometer to check the temperature of the melting wax.

● Keep your working area uncluttered and free from pets and children.

● Make sure that when you burn candles they are placed on a suitable surface away from inflammable materials and not left unattended.

● Leave wax spilt on fabric to harden before scraping it off, removing the remainder by ironing through a piece of kitchen towel.

● Scrape away wax spilt on wood then polish.

Using a Rigid Mould

For making candles at home, a wide range of rigid moulds are available in plastic, glass and metal. Whichever style of mould you choose to work with, make sure it is clean and dry before you begin. The basic technique is the same for all moulds: a primed wick is threaded into the mould, which is then filled with molten wax

1 Add a measured amount of stearin to the top of a double boiler and melt over a low heat. When the stearin has melted, add the dye and wait until it has dissolved. Carefully add paraffin wax. Heat gently until it reaches 71°C (160°F), then switch off the heat.

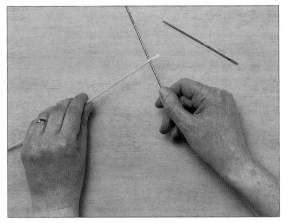

3 The coated end of the primed wick should always be at the burning end of the candle. When the wick is set hard, push a wicking needle, skewer or small knitting needle carefully through the other end of the primed wick.

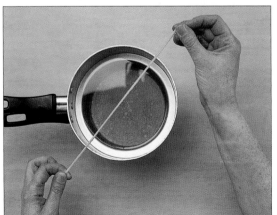

2 Cut a wick 5cm (2in) longer than the mould. Dip the wick into the molten wax for one minute. Straighten it between your fingers then lay it flat until set.

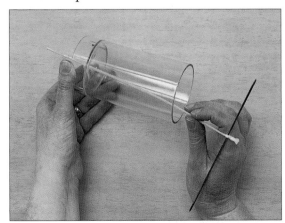

4 Using a wicking needle push the primed wick carefully up through the small hole in the end of the mould. Do not bend the wick or the wax coating will crack.

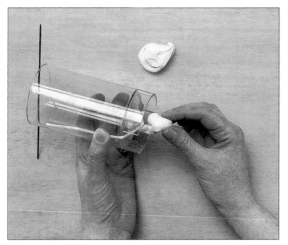

5 Lay the wicking needle over the open base of the mould. Pull the wick tightly back through the small hole at the top, holding the excess firmly against the outside surface of the mould. Secure the wick by covering the small hole with a lump of mould seal. Check that the seal is watertight by holding it under water. The wick should be central and straight in the mould.

6 Reheat the wax to 93°C (200°F). Transfer it to a pouring jug, checking the temperature constantly to make sure it is retaining the heat. Carefully pour the wax into the mould and fill to about 1.25cm (¹/₂in) from the top. Allow to cool for two minutes, then tap to release any air bubbles.

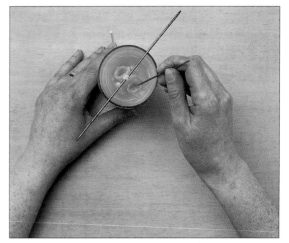

7 As the wax cools it will set from the bottom upwards, forming a conical shaped well around the wick. Under the skin the wax continues to cool and to shrink, forming a cavity below the surface. Break the skin with a wicking needle either side of the wick to gain access to the cavity. If the wax is still liquid inside, leave to cool for a few minutes longer.

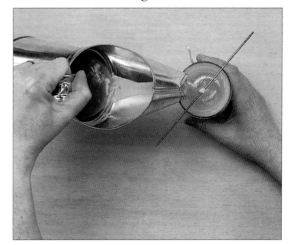

8 Reheat the wax to 93°C (200°F). Slowly top up the cavity with hot wax. Do not fill above the original level, or the candle will be difficult to remove from the mould. Wiggle the wick to allow all the air to escape from the cavity. Cool at room temperature, or in a water bath.

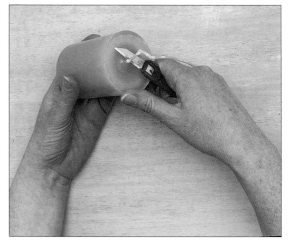

9 To speed up the cooling process stand the mould in a water bath. Use a large flat bottomed bowl, filled with enough cold water for the mould to stand upright and the water to be level with the top of the wax. Use a weight to keep the mould stable. Allow to cool for one hour. Water cooling will improve the appearance of the candle and make it easier to remove from the mould.

11 Remove the wicking needle from the top of the candle. Using a sharp craft knife carefully trim the wick flush with the base of the candle and 1.25cm ($\frac{1}{2}$in) above the top. Do not cut the wick any shorter or you may have trouble lighting the candle. Leave the top wick uncut if you are overdipping the candle. Remove all the mould seal from around the wick.

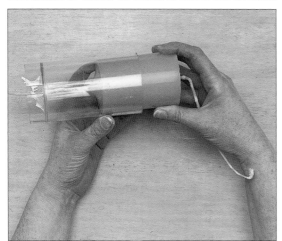

10 When the wax is completely cold, carefully peel away the mould seal from the bottom of the mould. Turn the mould the right way up and the candle will slide out into your hand. If you have trouble releasing the candle from the mould, turn to Candle Troubleshooting on page 62.

12 Flatten the base of the candle by heating it in a saucepan. Stand the candle in the clean, warm pan and move it around until the base is flat and the candle stands upright. Trim the wick again if necessary. The candle is now ready to be used, or over-dipped with another colour.

Candle Making Techniques

Although candle making can be expensive if you invest in glass or metal moulds, there is now a great deal of cheaper equipment available to the home candle maker. Rubber moulds are relatively inexpensive; or you may prefer to make your own from milk or juice cartons. Try dipping or making sand candles for spectacular results

Using a rubber mould

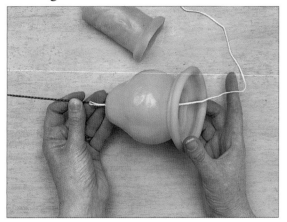

1 New moulds do not have a hole at the top for the wick, so make a small hole at the centre top with a wicking needle. Thread the needle and the wick up through the mould. Always use an unprimed wick so that the hole in the mould does not get too big.

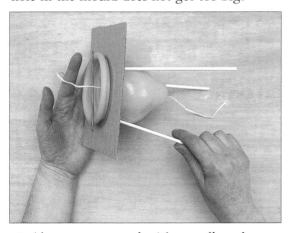

2 Always use a stand with a cardboard template at the neck to support the mould, and a wicking needle to support the wick. A jar can be used instead of the stand.

Making chunk candles

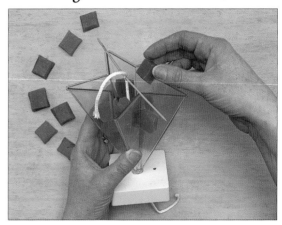

Fill the mould with wax chunks made from new wax or old candles. Pour the melted wax in a baking tray, when cold cut into chunks. Pour wax over the chunks in the mould.

Making votives

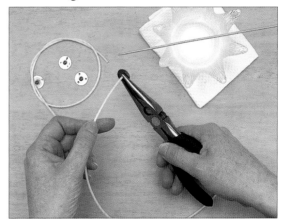

Tins, jars and old glass containers all make good votives. Use a wire or paper-cored wick fixed to a sustainer using pliers. Suspend the wick across the top on a wicking needle.

Making floating candles

Any mould can be used to make floating candles providing that the top is wider than the base, or it is wider than it is high: plastic sweet trays make good moulds. Pour melted wax into the mould, then as the wax is setting make a hole in the centre and push in a length of floating candle wick.

Making moulded candles

Modelling wax can be bought in packs ready to use. Soften in a bowl of warm water before using. Make your own modelling wax from dip-and-carve wax. Heat to 71°C (160°F), pour a layer on to baking parchment then model while the wax is warm. A hairdryer will soften hardening wax.

Making sand candles

1 Part fill a bucket with damp sand. Make an impression in the sand using a solid object: a block of wood, shell, metal can, or candle mould all make good indentations. Place a thermometer in the hole and pour wax over it: this will reduce the force with which the wax meets the sand. Continue until the indentation is full. Top up as the wax seeps into the sand.

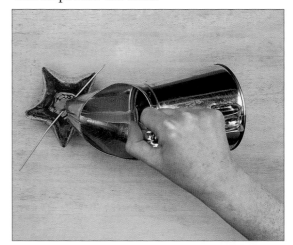

2 When the wax has set, remove the sand candle from the bucket. The sides will be covered in a layer of sand, and a well will have formed in the centre of the candle. Make a hole down through the middle and insert a primed wick. Top up the well with wax. Allow to cool then trim the wick.

Dipping and overdipping

1 Stand a dipping can or large clean food can in a saucepan of water; heat the water until the wax reaches a temperature of 71°C (160°F). Dip a pair of primed wicks into the hot wax for three seconds, cool for three minutes without letting the candles touch. Repeat several more times building up the thickness of wax. Increase the temperature to 82°C (180°F), dip the wicks, cool and repeat.

2 To overdip candles with another colour, melt wax and dye in the dipping can, heated to a temperature of 82°C (180°F). Dip the candle into the wax for three seconds, repeat until the candle is the right colour. To seal decorated candles, overdip in white wax for three seconds.

Pour-in pour-out candles

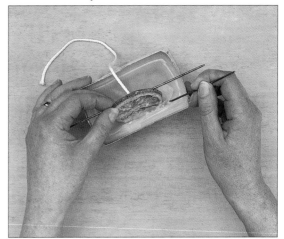

This pour-in pour-out method of candle making allows the candle to burn in the middle while the outer casing remains intact. Pour the wax into the mould; then as the candle is setting, push fruit slices against the sides of the container. After a short while, pour out the liquid wax and then refill.

Rolled beeswax candles

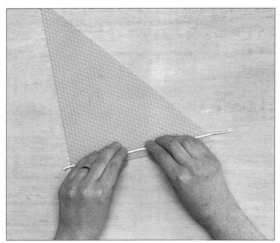

Beeswax sheets may need to be warmed to stop them cracking when rolled: use a heater or hairdryer to soften the wax. Lay the wick on the edge of a wax sheet and squeeze a small amount of wax around the protruding wick. Roll on a clean damp work surface, keeping the ends square and the roll even.

Stencilled Candles

Bring a fresh spring-like feel to plain candles using these simple flower stencils. The plain cream coloured candles are made in rigid moulds and then decorated with paint. If you would prefer not to make the candles, any straight-sided, pale coloured candle can be used to complete this project

You will need

- Paraffin wax – 1.5kg (3lb)
- Wax dye disc– cream
- Stearin – 150g (6oz)
- 5cm(2in) wick – 90cm (36in) long, for candles with a diameter larger than 5cm (2in)
- 3.75cm(1½in) wick – 18cm (7in) long, for candles with a diameter of 4cm (1½in)
- Rigid plastic moulds – cylindrical 22cm tall x 6.4cm diameter (8½x2½in), 18.5cm tall x 7cm diameter (7½x2¾in), 12cm tall x 4cm diameter (4¾x1½in), 11.4cm tall x 6cm diameter (4½x2¾in)
- Acrylic paint – bright green, leaf green, purple, lilac, cerise, yellow, orange
- Stencil film, craft knife, cutting mat, pencil
- Masking tape, washing-up liquid
- Sponge pieces, small paintbrush
- Flat dish for mixing paint, container of clean water, kitchen paper
- Double boiler, water bath
- Thermometer, scissors
- Mould seal, metal wicking needle

Melting the wax

1 Fill the bottom of a double boiler with water and place the upper saucepan on top.

2 Place the stearin and the cream dye in the top of the boiler and melt over a low heat. One dye disc will colour 2kg of wax so you will only need to use a small amount of the disc.

3 Carefully add the paraffin wax pellets and heat gently to 71°C (160°F) and until all the pellets have melted.

Priming the wick

1 While the wax is heating cut a piece of wick 5cm (2in) longer than the length of each mould. Dip the wick into the melted wax for one minute to prime it. Straighten the wick between your fingers then lay it flat to become hard. The wick can be primed before you start, or with the same wax as you are using to make the candles.

Wicking up

1 Using the wicking needle push the primed wick up through the small hole in the end of the mould. Push the wicking needle, skewer or small knitting needle through the primed wick then lay it across the open end of the mould. Pull the other end of the wick taught, securing it with a lump of mould seal (see Using a Rigid Mould, page 8). The hole must

be tightly sealed otherwise the hot wax will drip out of the mould. Make sure the wick is running centrally down through the mould. Check that the mould is watertight by holding it under water. Repeat for all the moulds.

Pouring the wax

1 Heat the wax to 93°C (200°F). Carefully pour the wax into the centre of each mould and fill up to about 1.25cm (1/2in) from the top.

2 After two minutes give the side of each mould a gentle tap with a spoon handle to dislodge any air bubbles. Candles will cool at room temperature, but you can speed up the time by standing each mould in a large bowl of cold water. When the mould is in the bowl the water should be level with the top of the wax. Use a weight to stop the mould floating.

3 As the wax starts to set a conical well will form around the wick. As it continues to cool it will shrink and form a cavity below the surface of the wax: break the skin with a needle to gain access to the cavity. If the wax is still liquid inside, replace the mould in the water bath until it begins to set.

4 Reheat the remaining wax to 93°C (200°F). Top up the cavity with hot wax. Do not fill above the original wax level. Return to the water bath and leave to cool for two hours.

5 Remove the seal and then turn the mould upside down allowing the candle to slide out. Trim the wick using a knife or scissors.

Tracing the stencil

1 Lay clear stencil film over the flower designs on the opposite page and carefully go over the design lines with a pencil. Place the stencil film on a cutting mat and hold with one hand. Using a sharp craft knife, and

following the design lines, start cutting from the centre of the design. Move the stencil as you cut, drawing the knife towards you. Where the individual parts of the design are close together or overlap, it may be easier to cut the stencil in more than one piece, like on the violets where one stencil should be cut for the leaves and another for the flowers.

Painting the candles

1 Wrap a stencil carefully around each candle and secure using tape.

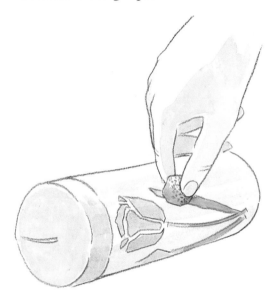

2 Mix each acrylic paint colour with a tiny spot of washing-up liquid: this will help the paint to adhere to the wax. The paint should be applied to the candle through the gaps cut in the stencil with a piece of sponge, using the photograph on page 15 as a guide. The colours will need to be built up using several layers of paint. Allow each layer to dry before adding more paint or removing the stencil. If the stencil has been cut in several parts, care should be taken when removing the first stencil and aligning the second so that it sits correctly over the partially painted design. Once the stencil has been removed use a fine paint-brush to add detail to the flowers.

Trace over the flower designs on to clear acetate, then
cut away the area inside the outlines to make stencils.

Glass Votives

Votives are the easiest of all candles to make. Scour junk shops and jumble sales for old pressed glass such as sugar bowls, jelly moulds, wine glasses or footed dishes. If you make the wax pale in colour, the glass containers will sparkle as the wax burns down

You will need
- Paraffin wax – 400g (15oz)
- Microcrystalline soft – 40g (1½oz)
- Wax dye disc – various colours
- Containers – glass, tin or terracotta
- Candle perfume
- Wire-cored or paper-cored wick
- Wick sustainers
- Skewer or wicking needle
- Mould seal
- Pliers
- Thermometer
- Double boiler

Preparing the containers

1 Votive candles can be made in any container that will withstand the heat of melted wax. Old pressed glass jelly moulds, terracotta plant pots, metal tins or jars make ideal containers. Check that the container does not leak, and if made from glass is not cracked. Wash the container thoroughly in hot soapy water and leave to dry. If you are using a plant pot with a drainage hole, block the hole at the bottom completely with a lump of mould seal.

2 To enable the candle to burn freely, the opening at the top of the container must not be less than 5cm (2in). As the candle burns the wax will be 'contained' creating an oil lamp effect: this can become heated above its flash point, so care should be taken not to leave candles unattended when burning, and to place them on a flat surface.

Choosing the wick

1 To allow the votives to burn off the excess wax, a wire-cored or paper-cored wick must be used. This must be held securely to the base of the container using a metal wick sustainer.

2 Cut a length of wick 5cm (2in) longer than the height of the votive. Wicks are graded in sizes: choose one that corresponds to the size of the container. The wick size will affect the way that the candle burns: if the wick is too

thick the candle will soot and smoke; if the wick is too thin it will not burn sufficiently.

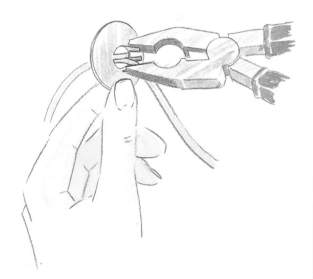

Securing the wick

1 Thread one end of the wire-cored or paper-cored wick through the hole in the metal wick sustainer. Using pliers, crimp the tabs on the sustainer around the wick, so that the wick is held securely in place (see Candle Making Techniques, page 11).

2 The wick must be held upright and taut by wrapping it around a skewer or small knitting needle, which is then laid across the top of the container. If you experience problems keeping the wick straight, use a small piece of mould seal to fix the wick sustainer to the bottom of the container.

Melting the wax

1 Fill the bottom of a double boiler with water and place the upper saucepan on top.

2 Place the paraffin wax into the top section of the double boiler. Use a thermometer to check the temperature of the wax. The wax will start to melt at about 60°C (140°F).

3 Add the microcrystalline soft and the dye carefully to the melting wax. The microcrystalline will make the wax more flexible and help it adhere to the sides of the container. Use ten parts of paraffin wax to one part microcrystalline soft. One dye disc will colour 2kg of wax so you will only need to use a small amount of the disc. Votives, especially if the containers are glass, are best filled with white, cream or pastel coloured wax. This will stop the wax colour overpowering the container.

4 Continue to melt the wax, microcrystalline and dye until it reaches a temperature of 82°C (180°F). Remove the double boiler from the heat source as soon as the temperature has been reached.

5 Stir in a few drops of perfume. A wide choice of candle fragrances are available, which are oil-soluble and specially formulated to be burnt. The best of these are the natural fruit and flower essences. To check what the candle will smell like when burnt: place a drop of essence on a length of wick, light it, then blow it out.

Filling the container

1 Pour the melted wax slowly into the centre of the container, making sure the wick stays central and fixed to the bottom. Do not fill the container right to the top, or it may spill over when the wax has melted.

2 After two minutes give the side of the container a gentle tap with a spoon handle to dislodge any air bubbles.

3 As the wax starts to set a conical well will form around the wick. As it continues to cool it will shrink and form a cavity below the surface of the wax: break the skin with a needle to gain access to the cavity. If the wax is still liquid inside, leave it to set.

4 Reheat the wax remaining in the double boiler to 82°C (180°F) and top up the cavity in the candle: do not fill above the original wax level.

5 Allow the votive to cool for two hours or until completely cold and set.

6 Remove the skewer and trim the wick to 1.25cm (1/2in) above the wax.

Rolled Beeswax Candles

These beautiful beeswax candles are made from preformed honeycomb sheets. Each candle takes just a few minutes to make, and is easy to decorate with bows, holly or stars cut from the same wax sheets. Why not give the candles as Christmas gifts, wrapped in paper and tied with a string bow?

Beeswax candles have a longer burning time than paraffin wax candles and a wonderful aroma.

You will need

- Beeswax sheets – natural or coloured
- Round braided wick – size according to finished diameter of candle
- Sharp craft knife, cutting board
- Scissors, metal ruler

Using beeswax sheets

1 Beeswax sheets are available in natural and a variety of colours. The preformed honeycomb sheets are approximately 30x20cm (12x8in) in size. The sheets are best worked at a warm room temperature; in cold weather they can be held near a heater or warmed very gently using a hair dryer until they become pliable. Roll the candles on a clean damp work surface or chopping board.

2 The size of the wick will depend on the diameter of the finished candle. Wicks are graded in sizes: choose one that corresponds to the diameter of the candle. A candle with a diameter of 25mm (1in) will require a 25mm (1in) size wick and a 50mm (2in) candle a wick size of 50mm (2in). Always use a round, braided wick for beeswax candles.

Making plain rolled candles

1 One full sheet of beeswax, rolled from the shortest edge, will produce a 2.5cm (1in) diameter candle. Lay a sheet of beeswax on to a damp surface, then cut a piece of wick 15mm (5/8in) longer than the length of the sheet.

2 Lay the wick along the shortest edge of the sheet, with one end protruding. From the bottom corner of the sheet, remove a small amount of wax. Squeeze the wax around the wick protruding at the top.

3 Carefully fold a small amount of the beeswax sheet over the wick along the shortest length (see Candle Making Techniques, page 13).

4 Roll up the sheet, keeping the ends square and the roll even.

5 For a thicker candle join in another sheet of beeswax by butting the edge of the existing sheet up to the new one. The height of candle can be altered by cutting the wax sheet with sharp craft knife before you begin rolling the candle up.

Chimney pot candle

1 Cut a piece of blue beeswax 30x9cm (12x3½in). Place a length of wick on the short edge of the sheet and roll up the candle.

2 Cut a second strip of blue beeswax 30x7cm (12x3in), butt the edges as before and roll up, keeping the bottom edge of the candle level. Add a third band of blue beeswax 5cm (2in) deep, in the same way as before.

3 The chimney pot candle will now have three different levels of the same coloured wax. Using the diagrams opposite as a guide: cut holly leaves from green beeswax, and make holly berries from balls of red beeswax. Warm the leaves and berries in your hands before pressing them on to the front of candle.

Making a multi-wick candle

1 Cut a sheet of natural beeswax into three strips each 30x7cm (12x3in) and make three candles of the same size and height, each with its own wick. Press the candles together in a triangular shape.

2 Cut two strips of natural beeswax 30x7cm (12x3in) wide. Roll the first strip around

the three candles. Butt the second strip to the first and finish rolling it around the candles: the three candles are now enclosed in a wax layer.

Making a star candle

1 Make a plain rolled candle using natural beeswax sheets cut to 10cm (4in) wide with a central wick. Continue joining the sheets and rolling until the candle is approximately 5cm (2in) in diameter. Mould the candle with your hands until the sides are flat and square.

2 Cut a strip of blue beeswax 10cm (4in) wide and long enough to fit around the candle. Using the star template opposite, cut a shape out of the beeswax strip.

3 Roll the strip around the candle, with the star cut-out in the middle of one side.

Christmas tree candle

1 Using the template opposite, cut eight Christmas trees from green beeswax. Press a length of wick between two tree shapes. Keep the wick central with 4cm (1½in) protruding below the bottom and 15mm (⅝in) at the top. Press three more tree shapes on either side of the first two.

2 Cut a piece of red beeswax sheet 4cm (1½in) wide and roll it around the length of wick protruding at the bottom of the tree to form the base. Trim the wick to 1.25cm (½in) and decorate the tree with tiny beeswax bows.

Making tapered candles

1 Tapered candles are made using a triangle instead of a rectangle of beeswax. Use a metal ruler and a sharp craft knife to cut the wax to size.

2 Place the wick on the edge as before, then carefully roll up the candle, keeping the bottom edges neat. As it is rolled the candle will taper down evenly. If the sheet runs out, cut another triangle and continue rolling until you reach the bottom of the candle. Trim the wick to 1.25cm (½in).

3 Tapered candles may be altered by varying the angle of the slope cut across the beeswax. If the cut goes between the opposite corners of the sheet, only one sheet will be needed, making a tall thin candle. For a thicker candle, cut a less steep angle, across several sheets of wax.

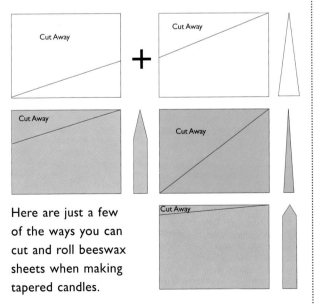

Here are just a few of the ways you can cut and roll beeswax sheets when making tapered candles.

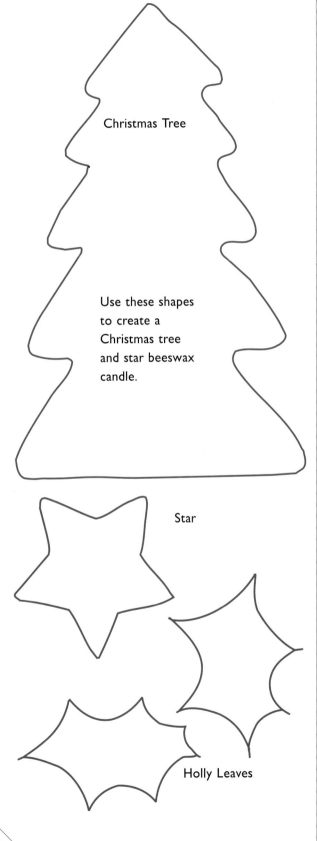

Christmas Tree

Use these shapes to create a Christmas tree and star beeswax candle.

Star

Holly Leaves

Hand Dipped Tapers

Hand dipping is one of the most rewarding ways to make candles; it is time consuming but the finished results are well worth the effort. Hand dipping is one of the simplest and oldest methods of making candles, although today most commercially dipped candles are made by machine

You will need

- Paraffin wax – 3kg (6lb 10oz) of wax will make approximately six tapers
- Wax dye discs – blue, pink and purple
- 1.25cm (½in) wick – 75cm (30in) long for each pair of candles
- Saucepan, water
- Dipping can 30cm (12in) tall
- Thermometer
- Craft knife
- Length of wood
- Rolling pin
- Greaseproof paper
- Scissors

Choosing your container

1 These straight and twisted tapers are made by dipping a wick into melted wax and building up the thickness of the wax around it. The dipping container will need to be tall enough to take the height of the finished taper. Any tall narrow metal or heatproof container can be used, as long as it will withstand the heat of the water and wax. The dipping can needs to be wide enough to hold two tapers side by side without the wicks touching. A large pet food tin will make a good dipping can; wash it thoroughly and then put it in the oven on a very low heat to dry before using.

Melting the wax

1 Stand the dipping can in a saucepan of water. Place the paraffin wax in the can and heat gently until the wax reaches 71°C (160°F). 3kg (6lb 10oz) of wax will make approximately six tapers, but the amount of wax needed will depend on the size of your dipping container. The depth of the melted wax in the can will control the finished length of your tapers.

2 Add a wax dye disc to the wax: three dye discs will give a very deep colour to 3kg (6lb 10oz) of wax. You can adjust the depth of colour by adding more or less dye. Test the colour by dropping a little melted wax on to a plate and allowing to cool completely.

Priming the wick

1 While the wax is heating cut a piece of wick 75cm (30in) long. Dip the wick into the melted wax for one minute to prime it. If you want the wick to be coated in white wax, prime it before you add the dye.

2 Straighten the wick between your fingers then fold it in half and hang it over a length of wood to cool. The tapers are dipped in pairs and the wick cut through at the top once the candles have cooled.

Making dipped tapers

1 With the temperature of the wax at 71°C (160°F), dip each pair of wicks into the melted wax for three seconds. Use your fingers to space the wicks apart and to keep them steady. Carefully lift the coated wicks from the dipping can; a layer of wax will have adhered to both lengths of wick. Allow the coated wicks to cool for approximately three minutes, without letting them touch. The pairs of tapers can be hung over a length of wood to cool between each dipping.

2 Check the temperature of the wax with a thermometer at regular intervals, keeping it at 71°C (160°F). Dip the tapers back into the

melted wax as before, cool and repeat several more times until the tapers are approximately 1.5-2cm (½-¾in) thick.

3 Once you are happy with the thickness of the tapers, increase the temperature of the wax to 82°C (180°F) and dip for three seconds, cool and repeat. This will give the tapers a smoother finish.

4 If you do have bumps on the surface of the tapers, the wax is probably not the correct temperature. Reheat the wax to 82°C (180°F), roll the warm tapers on your work surface to remove some of the bumps and re-dip.

5 Leave the tapers to cool slightly then trim the base of each flat. Cut through the wick between the two tapers and trim each to 6mm (¼in) above the wax.

Making flat twisted tapers

1 The tapers can only be twisted if the wax is still warm and pliable. Allow just 30 seconds for the wax to cool after the tapers have been removed from the dipping can before rolling. If the wax starts to crack, it will need to be warmed. Reheat the wax to 71°C (160°F) and dip the tapers for three seconds before rolling.

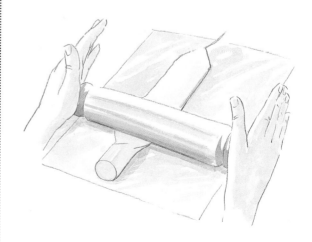

Making double twisted tapers

1 Twisted tapers can be made from white or coloured tapers; or white tapers over-dipped with coloured wax.

2 The dipped tapers need to be very warm to allow the twists to be made without the wax cracking. If the wax has hardened and has become unworkable, re-dip the tapers and leave for just 30 seconds before twisting together.

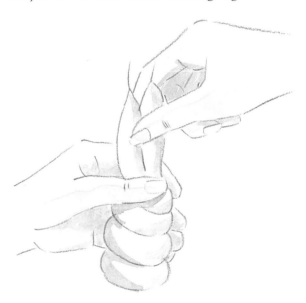

2 Make a pair of dipped tapers following the instructions on the previous page. Cut through the wick and lay one of the warm tapers on a piece of damp greaseproof paper. Using a wet rolling pin, roll over the taper until it is a thickness of about 6mm (¼in), leaving 5cm (2in) unflattened at the base to fit into a candle holder.

3 Holding the flattened taper upside down, twist the candle with your thumb and forefinger into a spiral.

4 Use a drawing pin to hang the taper up to cool, then trim the base flat and the wick to about 6mm (¼in) above the wax.

3 To make the white twisted tapers: dip the wicks until the tapers are thicker than before. The thick tapers will give extra shape to the finished candles. Holding the warm tapers firmly in your left hand, and with the tops level: twist the bottoms with your right hand in a clockwise direction, pressing down as you twist. This will make the candle more compact at the bottom.

4 To make the taller thinner twisted tapers: dip the wicks in coloured wax or over-dip white tapers with colour. Gently twist the two warm tapers together, keeping the turns long and even. Allow to cool then trim the wick to 1cm (⅜in).

Clown Candles

These fun birthday cake candles have been modelled using soft wax. The wax, which comes ready to use in multi-coloured packs, is softened in a bowl of hot water and then formed into shapes around a wick. So light the candles, bring on the cake, and let the party begin...

NOTE The candles will only burn for a short length of time and should not be left unattended.

You will need

- Soft modelling wax – one pack
- Wick, cocktail stick
- Craft knife, hairdryer
- White paper, ball-point pen
- Bowl of hot water, teaspoon
- Kitchen paper

Working with wax sheets

1 Soft modelling wax is supplied in packs of assorted coloured sheets. The pack contains several sheets of wax and a length of wick.

2 Remove the wax sheets from the wrapper and place them in a bowl of hand hot water to soften. After about five minutes, remove the wax sheets from the water and pat them dry using a sheet of kitchen paper. The wax sheets will become cold and unworkable very quickly, so they should be repeatedly returned to the hot water to keep them pliable. Warm air from a hairdryer will also keep the wax workable.

3 The colour of the wax sheets will depend on which pack you buy. Any combination of colours can be used to make the clown candles.

Making the clown's head

1 The diagrams on page 33 show the rough sizes of the clown's body parts. For the head, roll a piece of wax into a 2cm (³⁄₄in) ball. Push a cocktail stick down through the centre to take the wick.

2 Cut a length of wick 8cm (3in) long. Feed the wick down through the head, leaving 3cm (1¹⁄₄in) protruding from the top. Gently roll the ball around, to help fix the wick in place. Do not cut the wick, as it will need to be threaded down through the body later.

Making the body

1 Mould a piece of wax into a fat sausage shape until it resembles the template for the body on the opposite page.

2 Make a hole in one end of the body using a cocktail stick. Push the wick that is protruding from the bottom of the clown's head down into the hole in the body. Mould the head and the body together. If the wax does not stick together, return the wax to the hot water or use a hairdryer to soften it.

Making the arms and legs

1 For the arms mould two pieces of wax into sausage shapes about 2.5cm (1in) long. Press the arms in place either side at the top of the body.

2 The legs are formed by moulding two pieces of wax into sausage shapes about 3cm (1¼in) long. Fix in place at the base of the

body, so that the legs act as supports for the sitting clown.

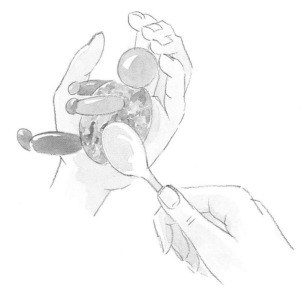

3 If you have difficulty securing the arms and legs to the body, the wax can be softened by pressing a hot teaspoon against the parts to be stuck together.

Making the hands and feet

1 Roll two balls of wax for the hands and two for the feet, and attach them to the ends of the arms and legs.

Making the hair

1 Roll out a piece of wax to a thickness of about 3mm ($^1/_8$in). Trace over the template for the hair on to white paper and cut out the shape. Lay the template on top of the wax, then using a craft knife cut out the hair.

2 Mould the hair around the crown of the clown's head and press gently in place.

Adding the features

1 For the eyes and nose roll balls of coloured wax and press them on to the face.

2 Make the mouth by rolling a tiny sausage shape and pressing it on to the face.

Finishing the clown

1 Using the photograph on page 32 as a guide, make a hat by moulding a small piece of wax into a cone shape. Make a hole in the top of the hat by pushing a cocktail stick down through the centre. Feed the wick from the top of the head up through the hat. Mould the hat on to the head and trim the wick to 1cm ($^1/_2$in).

2 The shape of the hat can be varied by adding a sausage shaped brim around the bottom of the hat; making a tall conical shaped hat decorated with small coloured wax balls; or by sitting the hat on a flat circle of wax and then passing the wick through both the brim and the hat.

3 Decorate the hat and front of the clown's tunic with balls, stars, triangles and feathers cut and shaped from coloured wax.

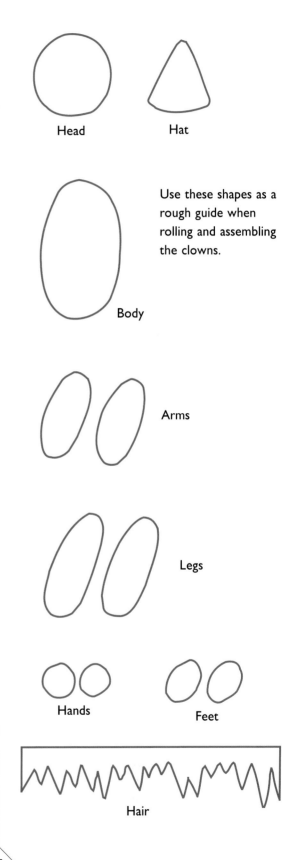

Head

Hat

Use these shapes as a rough guide when rolling and assembling the clowns.

Body

Arms

Legs

Hands

Feet

Hair

Chunk Candles

These attractive multi-coloured candles are made in rigid moulds by pouring hot wax over chunks of cold wax. As the wax flows over the chunks they begin to melt leaving colour trails in the candle. The chunks can be made from left over candle ends or by pouring a thin layer of wax into a baking tray

You will need

- Paraffin wax – 2kg (4lb)
- Stearin – 200g (8oz)
- Wax dye discs – orange, green, yellow
- Rigid mould – cylindrical 17.5x7cm (7x2¾in), pyramid 22x6cm (8½x2¼in), pyramid 16x16cm (6½x6½in), five pointed star 11.5x11.5cm (4½x4½in)
- 5cm (2in) wick – 75cm (30in) long
- Baking tray, foil, two teaspoons
- Thermometer, mould seal
- Metal wicking needle, skewer or knitting needle
- Double boiler
- Egg poacher or two clean tins and a saucepan
- Electric iron, white spirit, newspaper

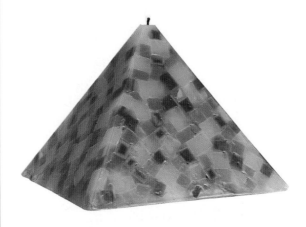

Making the chunks

1 To create the marbled effect in the chunk candles, you need to pour dye over lumps of wax. Old candles can be recycled by cutting them into chunks of about 1.25-2.5cm (½-1in); or you can make your own from stearin and wax pellets. Tip paraffin wax pellets into a foil covered baking sheet to a depth of 1.25cm (½in). Weigh the pellets, allowing 10% of stearin to wax.

2 Place the stearin in the top of a double boiler and melt over a low heat. If you are making coloured chunks, add the dye and wait until it has dissolved. One wax disc will colour 2kg of wax so you will only need a small portion of each disc to colour a tray of wax.

3 Carefully add the paraffin wax pellets and heat gently to 82°C (180°F). Pour the melted wax into the foil lined baking tray. Allow the tray to cool then break the wax into pieces. If you are making chunks for the large pyramid candle, cut the cooled wax into even squares using a knife.

Priming the wick

1 Heat a small amount of wax in a double boiler until it reaches a temperature of 71°C (160°F). Turn off the heat. Cut a piece of wick 5cm (2in) longer than the mould. Dip the wick in the melted wax for one minute to prime it.

Straighten the wick between your fingers then lay it flat to become hard. The wick can be primed before you start, or with the same wax as you are using to make the candles.

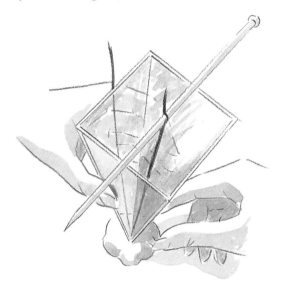

Wicking up

1 Using a wicking needle push the primed wick up through the small hole in the end of the mould. Push the wicking needle, skewer or small knitting needle through the primed wick then lay it across the open end of the mould. Pull the other end of the wick taught, securing it with a lump of mould seal.

2 The hole must be tightly sealed otherwise the hot wax will drip out of the mould. Make sure that the wick is taught and running centrally down through the mould. Test the mould to see if it is watertight by standing it in a bowl of water.

Marbled chunk candle

1 Wick up the pyramid or five pointed star mould then pack chunks of white wax around the wick.

2 Break off small pieces of yellow and orange, or yellow and green dye and heat them over

water in the egg poacher. If you do not have an egg poacher you can use clean, dry tin cans. These will need to float in a saucepan of water without falling over or touching the bottom. The dye should be warmed just enough to melt it.

3 Add 10g (⅓oz) of stearin to a saucepan and melt over a low heat. When melted add 90g (3¼oz) of paraffin wax and, using the thermometer, bring the wax up to 127°C (261°F). Remove from the heat immediately the temperature is reached. It is very important that you do not leave the wax unattended as it can ignite. Raise the temperature slowly, monitoring it continuously.

4 Pour the melted wax slowly into the mould allowing it to run around the chunks.

5 Using a teaspoon, pick up a little of the orange or green melted dye and add drops to the mould. Repeat with the yellow dye using a clean teaspoon. Leave the candle for about 45 seconds to allow the dye colours to swirl together. Candles will cool at room temperature, but you can speed up the time by standing the mould in a large bowl of cold water. When the mould is in the bowl the water should be level with the top of the wax. Use a weight to stop the mould floating.

6 As the wax starts to set a conical well will form around the wick. As it continues to cool it will shrink and form a cavity below the surface of the wax: break the skin with a needle to gain access to the cavity. If the wax is still liquid inside, replace the mould in the water bath until it begins to set (see Using a Water Bath, page 10).

7 Reheat the remaining wax to 93°C (200°F). Top up the cavity with hot wax. Do not fill

above the original wax level. Return to the water bath and leave to cool for two hours.

8 Remove the seal and then turn the mould upside down allowing the candle to slide out. Trim the wick using a knife or scissors.

Cubed pyramid candle

1 Prepare the mould by wicking up as before. Make trays of coloured wax in orange, green and yellow. Using a sharp knife cut the cold wax into even cubes making the orange and green chunks slightly smaller than the yellow. Fill the wicked mould with chunks pressing them tightly into the mould.

2 Melt 50g (2oz) of stearin and add ¼ of a yellow wax dye disc to the double boiler. When melted add 500g (1lb) of paraffin wax. Heat to 93°C (200°F) and pour slowly into the

mould. Allow the melted wax to fill the cavities around the chunks. Cool, top up and then trim the wick in the same way as before.

Melted chunk candle

1 Wick up the cylindrical mould. Make orange and green wax chunks and place in the mould.

2 In the double boiler melt 20g (²⁄₃oz) stearin and ⅛ orange dye disc. Add 200g (7oz) of wax and heat to 93°C (200°F). Pour into the mould. Cool and finish as before.

3 Working over newspaper or a saucepan, press an electric iron on a medium setting against the sides of the candle to form pits in the surface. Polish the sides of the candle with white spirit and then buff with a wet tissue to give the surface a shine.

Jewelled Candles

These jewelled candles make a stunning centre piece for a dinner party. Shapes cut from appliqué wax have been stuck on to plain white candles and then jewellery stones added for that extra bit of sparkle. Co-ordinate the look by decorating the candle holders and napkin rings with the same jewels

The gold appliqué wax used in this project can be burnt, but the jewels and studs should be removed before lighting the candles.

You will need

- Paraffin wax – 1.5kg (3lb)
- Stearin – 150g (5oz)
- Appliqué wax sheets – two metallic gold, two round gold strips, two holographic gold
- Appliqué wax lengths – gold
- 5cm(2in) wick – 60cm (25in) long
- 3.75cm(1½in) wick – 45cm (18in) long
- Rigid plastic moulds – cylindrical 22cm tall x 3cm diameter (8½x1¼in), 18.5cm tall x 7cm diameter (7½x2¾in), 12cm tall x 4cm diameter (4¾x1½in), 11.4cm tall x 6cm diameter (4½x2¼in), 16cm tall x 6cm square (6½x2¼x2¼in)
- Small pearl beads, jewel coloured plastic beads, flat backed jewellery stones
- Brass upholstery studs, star shaped pastry cutter,
- Double boiler, water bath, pin, sticky tape
- Thermometer, scissors, craft knife, tweezers
- Mould seal, metal wicking needle

Making the candles

1 To make the plain white candles used in this project, follow the candle making instructions for Stencilled Candles on page 14, omitting the cream dye.

Using appliqué wax

1 Lay white paper over the templates on page 41. Trace over the designs using a soft pencil. You can use a photocopier if you need to enlarge or reduce the design to fit the candles.

2 The appliqué wax sheets are self adhesive and supplied on a paper backing sheet. They are manufactured in sheets of metallic gold and silver; and in long thin strips for wrapping around candles. They should be cut using a very sharp craft knife, and only removed from their backing sheet when they are ready to be positioned on the candle. The wax used for the sheets is much softer than candle wax, so great care should be taken not to scratch the surface. After cutting, peel the shapes off the backing sheet and press firmly on to the candle. If you have problems getting the appliqué wax to stick: warm the candle and the wax for a few minutes before using.

Decorating the daisy candle

1 Make a tracing of the daisy template on page 41, extending the design to fit the candle. Wrap the tracing around the candle

Fruit Candles

Arranged in a bowl, fruit candles make a very realistic display. They are almost indistinguishable from the real thing and make wonderful presents. Made in a rubber mould, the wax is perfumed and then specially coloured using a super dye disc, ensuring that you get realistic coloured fruit every time

You will need

- Paraffin wax – 240g (9½oz) for each fruit
- Wax dye super disc for fruit candles – apple, orange, lemon or pear
- 3.75cm (1½in) wick – 15cm (6in) length for each fruit
- Perfume – apple, orange, lemon or pear
- Flexible rubber mould – apple, orange, lemon or pear
- Poster paint – burnt sienna
- Wicking needle, scissors
- Stiff cardboard template – 20x20cm (8x8in)
- Paintbrush, craft knife, cloth, white spirit
- Water bath, washing-up liquid
- Thermometer
- Double boiler, egg poacher
- Stand

Preparing the mould

1 If you are using a new rubber mould, a hole must be made at the end of the mould for the wick. Make a small hole with the wicking needle, then thread the unprimed wick up through the mould. Do not use a primed wick, or the hole may get too big and hot wax seep out (see Candle Making Techniques, page 11).

2 Cut a circle of stiff cardboard, with a hole in the centre large enough to hold the neck of the mould. Push the neck up through the hole in the card.

3 Support the mould on a mould stand, tin can, jar or jug. Take care that the mould is not touching the equipment or it will be pushed out of shape.

4 Thread the wicking needle through the wick at the open end of the mould then support the needle by laying it across the top of the mould. Gently pull the wick tight from the bottom.

Melting the wax

1 Fill the bottom of a double boiler with water and place the upper saucepan on top.

2 For each candle, place the wax and 3g, or ¹/₇ of a dye super disc in the top of the boiler and melt over a low heat. The super disc

contains colour and a dual purpose additive which enhances the density, aids burning and gives the fruit a realistic appearance.

3 Heat the wax and dye gently to 93°C (200°F) and until all the pellets have melted. Always use a thermometer to check the temperature of the melting wax. When the temperature has been reached, remove the double boiler from the heat. Add a few drops of perfume to the melted wax and stir well.

Using a water bath

1 While the wax is melting prepare a water bath to cool the fruit candle: this will improve the appearance of the candle and aid mould release. Almost any large bowl can be used, provided it is deep enough to take the mould and there is no more than 5cm (2in) of water around the mould.

2 Fill the water bath with cold water to within 1cm (½in) of the top of the mould. Remember that when you immerse the filled mould the level of the water will rise.

3 Do not have the water too cold as it may cause the wax to crack. Ideally the temperature should be between 10-15°C (50-59°F). Use a heavy weight to stop the filled mould floating in the water.

Filling the mould

1 Pour the melted wax into the mould and leave for one minute. Lift the mould up by its cardboard template and gently tap the sides with your finger to release any air bubbles that have formed around the wick. Lower the mould gently into the water bath.

2 As soon as the surface of the wax starts to solidify, a conical well will form around the wick and a cavity will form below the surface.

Break the skin with a wicking needle every fifteen minutes throughout the cooling period to release air bubbles.

3 After ten minutes, change the water in the bath. Do this twice more at ten minute intervals.

4 Leave the wax to cool for an hour and a half. Reheat the wax remaining in the double boiler to 93°C (200°F) and top up the cavity in the candle: do not fill above the original wax level. Carefully lift the mould out of the bath and allow to cool for at least one hour.

Removing the mould

1 Remove the cardboard template from the neck of the mould. If wax has leaked out through the wick hole, remove any lumps that have formed on the outer surface of the mould.

2 Cover the outside of the mould with neat washing-up liquid, then peel back the mould on itself to remove the candle.

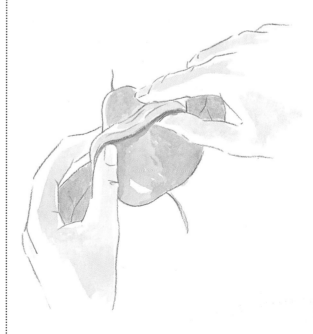

3 Cut the wick flat at the base of the candle, and shape the candle base until it stands flat on the work surface.

Finishing the pear candles

1 The pear candle needs to be painted to give a mottled finish to the skin. Mix together a little water, burnt sienna poster paint and a drop of washing-up liquid. Paint the outside of the pear with the mixture and allow to dry. To give a stippled finish polish off any excess colour with a cloth dipped in white spirit.

2 Overdip the candle for four seconds, in pale green or yellow wax heated to a temperature of 82°C (180°F). Wait one minute, then re-dip for two seconds. After fifteen minutes, polish the candle with a wet tissue.

Priming the wick

1 At this point, although the wicks can be trimmed and the candles burnt, you may prefer to coat each wick with coloured wax.

2 Small amounts of wax can be successfully heated in an egg poacher using the same method for the double boiler. Add the dye to the wax and then heat gently to melting point. Use brown dye for the apple, pear and orange and pale yellow for the lemon.

3 Trim each wick then dip into the hot wax. Bend the wick, on the pear and apple, gently into an arch shape over the top of the candle. For the orange candle, coil the wick in the centre of the candle. To burn the orange candle, open the wick up using a knife.

Sand Candles

Sand candles are one of the most creative types of candle. There can be no greater pleasure than creating a beautiful candle from shapeless sand and a metal bucket. As the candle burns, so the light will change the colour of the sand, creating a magical glow around the wax

You will need

- Paraffin wax – 475g (17oz)
- Wax dye – ¼ disc
- Stearin – 47.5g (2oz)
- 5cm (2in) wick – 75mm (3in) long
- Bucket
- Sand
- Water
- Saucepan
- Thermometer
- Metal wicking needle
- Mould for impression
- Coarse file, geometry dividers
- Modelling tool, craft knife

Choosing the mould

1 The shape of sand candles can be varied by using different shaped moulds to make an impression in wet sand. The indentation left in the sand will be the shape of the finished candle. Almost anything can be used as a mould, as long as it has a solid structure for pushing into the sand: a block of wood, shell, metal can or a shaped candle mould are just a few of the things that make good indentations.

2 The finished candle will be the same shape as the impression, with sand adhering to the sides, forming a decorative crusty coating. You can only produce one candle from each impression but the sand can be re-used. Fine, building or coarse sand with grit or small pebbles can be used, with each producing a different coloured and textured coating on the surface of the candle.

Preparing the sand

1 The sand needs to be damp, but not wet, in order to retain the impression left by the mould. It will take approximately 140ml (¼pt) of water to dampen half a bucket of sand. Add the water a little at a time to stop the sand becoming over wet, then stir thoroughly.

Making the mould

1 Pack at least 7.5cm (3in) of sand into the bottom of the bucket and press down

firmly. Place your chosen mould on top of the sand, then carefully pack more sand around its sides to the required height of the candle. For the star shaped candle, use a shell or a star shaped rigid candle mould if you have one.

2 Tap the bucket sharply on the floor to ensure that the sand is tightly packed around the mould.

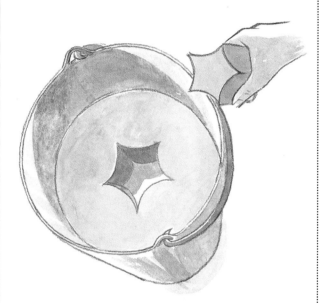

3 Level the sand and then carefully remove the mould, taking care not to knock any sand from the sides into the indented shape (see Candle Making Techniques, page 12). This will leave a hollow impression that can be filled with melted wax. If you are unhappy with the shape, level the sand and try again.

Melting the wax

1 To allow the hot wax to seep into the sand, a higher temperature than is normally needed to make candles must be reached. To achieve this higher temperature the wax will need to be melted in a saucepan. Place the stearin and the dye in the saucepan and melt over a low heat. A quarter of one dye disc will be enough to colour one candle.

2 Carefully add the paraffin wax pellets, and using the thermometer, bring the wax slowly up to 71°C (160°F).

Priming the wick

1 While the wax is heating cut a piece of wick 5cm (2in) longer than the height of the indentation. Dip the wick into the melted wax for one minute to prime it. Straighten the wick between your fingers then lay it flat to become hard. The wick can be primed before you start, or with the same wax as you are using to make the candle.

Pouring the wax

1 Using a thermometer, continue heating the wax to 127°C (261°F). Remove the saucepan from the heat immediately the temperature is reached, as if left to get too hot the wax can ignite (see Common Sense with Wax, page 7).

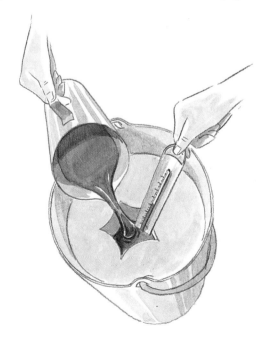

2 Place the thermometer in the indentation made in the sand, and pour the wax over the thermometer, allowing it to run into the hole. This will reduce the force with which the wax meets the sand, and help to stop the sand

falling into the indentation. Continue pouring until full. Remove the thermometer.

3 After about three minutes some of the wax will have seeped into the sand. Reheat the wax to 127°C (261°F) and refill the mould.

4 Leave the candle to set for several hours before removing it from the sand. The wax should be set, but still soft enough in the centre to make a hole with the wicking needle. Sand candles do take much longer than moulded candles to set, this is because the sand acts as an insulator, stopping the wax from cooling. Remove some of the sand from the bucket and carefully lift out the candle.

Wicking up the candle

1 A deep well will have formed in the centre of the candle, and the wax will have dropped below the sand coating on the sides. Push a wicking needle down through the middle of the candle, without penetrating the sand layer at the bottom.

2 Insert the primed wick into the hole made in the candle, and then support it at the top by wrapping it around the wicking needle, skewer or a knitting needle which is then carefully laid across the top of the candle.

3 Reheat the remaining wax to 104°C (219°F) and use it top up the well around the wick. Allow the candle to cool for several hours.

Finishing the candle

1 Remove the wicking needle, skewer or knitting needle and trim the wick using a craft knife or scissors.

2 Smooth the outer surface of the candle using a coarse file or rough sand paper.

Making a decorative pattern

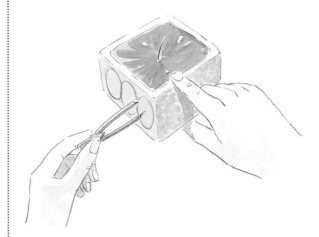

If you have made a flat sided candle, you may wish to mark out a decorative pattern in the sand. Using geometry dividers, scratch out a series of circles in the sand then carve away some parts of the sand using a modelling tool.

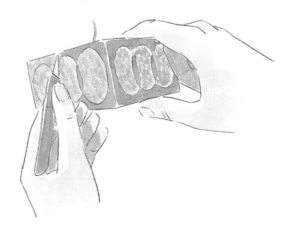

Moon and Star Candles

These celestial candles are made from white candles which have been overdipped using blue wax. A pattern is then cut in the blue wax, allowing the white wax to show through. The candles are then decorated with moon and star shapes cut from appliqué wax sheets, stencilled stars and gold eyelets

You will need

- Paraffin wax – 1.5kg (3lb) for candles
- Stearin – 150g (6oz)
- Paraffin wax – 1kg (2lb) for overdipping
- Wax dye discs – blue
- Appliqué wax sheets – lilac, blue, holographic gold, round gold strip
- Rub on metallic paste – gold, sapphire
- 5cm(2in) wick – 90cm (36in) long
- Rigid plastic moulds – cylindrical 9.5cm tall x 6cm diameter (3³/₄x2¹/₄in) 17.5cm tall x 7cm diameter (7x2³/₄in) 15cm tall x 5cm (6x2in) pyramid 22cm tall x 6cm base (8¹/₂x2¹/₄in)
- Eyelets – brass, black
- Pin, sticky tape, self adhesive stars
- Double boiler, water bath, dipping can
- Thermometer, scissors, craft knife
- Mould seal, metal wicking needle
- White paper, pen, greaseproof paper

Making the candles

1 To make the candles used for this project, follow the candle making instructions for Stencilled Candles on page 14, omitting the cream dye, and using rigid cylindrical and pyramid shaped moulds. Do not trim the wick at the top, as this can be used to hold the candle when overdipping.

Overdipping the candles

1 Once the large white candles are cold they can be coloured by overdipping in hot wax. The amount of paraffin wax needed will depend on the size of your dipping can: it will need to be wider than the candle and contain enough melted wax to cover the whole of the candle when immersed. Stand the dipping can in a large saucepan of water (see Candle Making Techniques, page 13).

2 Place the paraffin wax in the dipping can and melt until it reaches 82°C (180°F), then add the blue wax dye disc. One disc will colour 1kg (2lb) of paraffin wax to a deep blue.

3 Dip the candle into the hot wax, count to three, remove the candle then allow to cool for 30 seconds. Repeat the dipping several times until the candle are deep blue. The wax must remain at a constant 82°C (180°F): if the wax is too hot it will not adhere to the candle. Allow to cool before decorating.

Candle carving

1 To enable the blue wax on the overdipped candle to be cut into a pattern, it must be the consistency of a wax skin on a cheese. Leave the candle for several days to allow the overdipped wax to set hard.

2 Trace over the geometric square and the outer star templates on page 53 on to white paper and cut out the shapes. Lay the geometric tracing around the base of the candle, using sticky tape to hold it in place.

3 Using a sharp pin, make a prick at each angle around the design. Lift off the tracing and repeat several times around the candle. If you are using a larger or smaller candle you will need to enlarge or reduce the design to fit around the candle.

4 Holding a ruler between two pin marks, cut through the blue wax layer with a craft knife. Do not press too hard or you will also cut into the white wax.

5 Remove the cut areas of blue wax to reveal the white wax beneath. Repeat around the bottom of the candle.

6 Lay the outer geometric star in the centre of the candle between the top and bottom patterns. Mark the shape as before, then remove the blue wax layer. Repeat around the middle of the candle.

7 Make a tracing of the diamond and inner star templates on page 53, and cut out the shapes. Lay the tracings on to a holographic gold appliqué sheet. Cut around the edges of the design, peel off the wax shapes and press on to the candle, using the photograph on page 51 as a guide.

8 Buff the candle gently with a piece of old stocking to remove any loose wax and fingerprints.

Moon and stars candle

1 Leave the overdipped blue candle to cool for several hours. Make a tracing of the star and moon templates on page 53 and cut out the shapes.

2 Place the sun and moon tracings on to a holographic gold appliqué sheet and cut around the design using a craft knife. Cut enough shapes to decorate the candle. Using the photograph on page 51 as a guide, peel the shapes from backing paper and press firmly on to the candle. Position a piece of round gold appliqué strip around the top of the candle.

Pyramid candles

1 Allow the white pyramid candles to cool for several hours. Make a tracing of the geometric steps, outer geometric star and diamond templates on page 53 and cut out the shapes.

2 To decorate the two pyramid candles you will need to cut the following shapes from appliqué wax sheets: four gold, two lilac, two

blue geometric steps; four gold, two lilac, two blue outer geometric stars; four gold, two lilac, two blue diamonds.

3 Peel the backing paper from the outer geometric stars one at a time and position them on the sides of the candles, following the photograph on page 51 for position. The diamond shapes should be placed in the middle of the geometric stars. Press a brass eyelet into the centre of each diamond.

4 Position the geometric steps on to the candle and press in place, lining up the straight edge of the wax with the sides of the candle. Repeat on all sides, alternating the colours. Press three eyelets down the centre of each step following the photograph on page 51 for position.

Star candle

1 Attach self-adhesive paper stars randomly over a white candle. Using your finger or a piece of cloth, apply gold and blue rub on metallic paste over each star shape, so that the colour spreads out on to the candle. Peel off the star shape to reveal the white wax beneath.

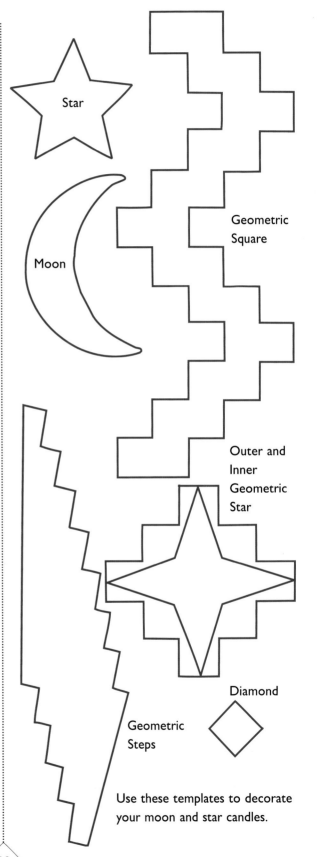

Star

Moon

Geometric Square

Outer and Inner Geometric Star

Diamond

Geometric Steps

Use these templates to decorate your moon and star candles.

Floating Candles

There is nothing more magical than the light produced from a bowl of floating candles. Almost any glass bowl can be used, as long as there is enough water for the candles to float freely. Add colouring, glitter, glass beads and marbles to give the water that extra special sparkle

You will need

- Paraffin wax – 225g (9oz)
- Stearin – 23g (³/₄oz)
- Floating candle wick
- Dip-and-carve wax – 500g (1lb)
- 1.25cm (¹/₂in) wick – 10cm (4in) length for each candle
- Wax dye discs – pink, blue, yellow, violet
- Candle perfume
- Plastic floating candle moulds
- Scissors, knife
- Baking parchment, white paper
- Thermometer, metal jug
- Double boiler

Choosing your mould

1 Almost any mould can be used to make floating candles provided that the top is wider than the base. Any small amount of left over wax can be used, and any unburnt candles remelted and poured into moulds.

Making moulded candles

1 Fill the bottom of a double boiler with water and place the upper saucepan on top.

2 Place the stearin and a small amount of wax dye in the top of the boiler and melt over a very low heat.

3 Carefully add the paraffin wax pellets and heat gently to 93°C (200°F), using a thermometer to check the temperature.

Adding the perfume

1 Once the wax has reached the correct temperature, remove the double boiler from the heat. Stir a few drops of perfume into the wax. A wide range of candle fragrances are available, which are oil-soluble and specially formulated to be burnt. A 15ml (5oz) bottle of perfume is sufficient to scent 4kg of wax so only a few drops will be needed. Too much perfume can cause mottling and pitting in the wax. To check what the candle will smell like when burnt: place a drop of essence on a length of wick, light it, then blow it out.

Pouring the wax

1 Pour the hot wax carefully into the moulds. As the wax is starting to solidify make a hole in the centre of each candle.

2 Cut a length of wick for each candle, 3cm (1½in) longer than the height of the mould. Insert a wick into each hole and leave the candle to cool. As the wax begins to harden, gently pull the wick upright.

3 Reheat the wax remaining in the double boiler and top up the candles to their original level. When completely cold remove each candle from the mould and trim the wick to 1cm (½in) above the candle. Allow to cool for at least 2 hours before lighting.

Making floating roses

1 Trace over the petal templates on page 57 on to white paper and cut out the shapes. Fill the bottom of a double boiler with water and place the upper saucepan on top.

2 Break up the dip-and-carve wax and place it in the top of the double boiler. Gently heat to 71°C (160°F), using the thermometer to check the temperature.

3 Add a small amount of the pink dye disc to the melted wax and stir until thoroughly mixed. Check the colour by dropping a little of the melted wax on to a clean dish and allow to cool. If the colour is too pale add a little more dye to the melted wax. Remove the double boiler from the heat source as soon as the correct temperature has been reached.

4 Add a few drops of candle perfume to the wax. Cut several lengths of wick and dip each in the melted wax for 1 minute to colour them. Floating candles use a special wax covered wick that is already primed, but for

the rose candles the wicks are overdipped in pink wax. Straighten each wick after it has been dipped and lay it on a flat surface to dry.

Moulding the petals

1 Lay a sheet of baking parchment on to your work surface. Tip some of the melted wax into the metal jug and pour a 3mm (⅛in) thick layer of wax on to the parchment. The working time of the wax is approximately ten minutes, so pour areas no larger than 15x15cm (6x6in). Allow the wax to cool for a very short while, until it becomes rubbery in texture. If the wax is left too long it will become hard and brittle; if it is too soft the top surface of wax will come off on your fingers when you are moulding the petals.

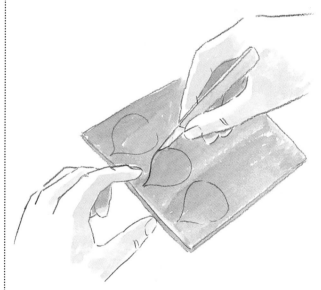

2 Lay a petal template on top of the wax and cut around the edge with a knife. Form a curved edge on the petals by the moulding wax between your fingers. A hairdryer can be used to soften the hardening wax.

3 Dip the end of a small petal into the melted wax and squeeze it around the middle of a primed wick leaving spare wick protruding from either end. Repeat with another small

petal. It is easier to form the centre of several roses and allow them to harden before adding the larger petals (see Techniques, page 12).

4 Place any wax left over after cutting the smaller petals back into the double boiler and remelt. Pour out more wax on to the baking parchment and cut larger petals adding them to the rose centres in the same way as before. Build up the roses, making the petals larger and curving the edges as you move outwards. Make sure the petals are firmly fixed to the base of the rose.

5 Trim off the wick at the base and to about 1cm (½in) at the top. Dip the base of the rose into melted wax to seal the bottom, then stand in an egg cup to cool. This will support

Use these shapes for cutting rose petals from the wax.

the petals whilst the wax is still soft and pliable. Allow to cool for two hours before placing in a bowl of water, deep enough to allow the flowers to float freely.

Natural Candles

Fruit, gravel and glass beads have been set inside these natural looking candles which have been made in old waxed fruit juice, milk or yogurt cartons. The appliquéd candles are made in the conventional way using rigid moulds; after decorating they are overdipped in wax to seal the surface

You will need
- Paraffin wax – 3.5kg (7lb)
- Stearin – 350g (14oz)
- 5cm(2in) wick – 120cm (48in) long
  3.75cm(1½in) wick – 18cm (7in) long
- Rigid moulds – cylindrical 22cm tall x 6.4cm diameter (8½x2½in), 18.5cm tall x 7cm diameter (7½x2¾in), 12cm tall x 4cm diameter (4¾x1½in), 11.4cm tall x 6cm diameter (4½x2¼in)
- Wax dye disc – orange
- Waxed cartons – orange juice, yogurt
- Chicken wire, rubber bands, wire cutters
- Glass beads, washed 10mm gravel
- Candle perfume – orange, apple
- Double boiler, water bath
- Dried fruit slices, petals and leaves, shells, mosaic tiles, chicken wire, gravel
- Thermometer, scissors, dipping can
- Mould seal, metal wicking needle, wick sustainers
- Rub on metallic paste – gold
- Lolly stick or skewer, blu-tack

Making the plain candles
1 To make the plain white candles used for applique, follow the candle making instructions for Stencilled Candles, on page 14, omitting the cream dye and leaving the candle wick several inches long at the top.

Making appliquéd candles
1 Collect leaves and petals, making your selection on a dry day, then press them overnight between the pages of a heavy book. Lay a plain white candle on its side and then place a selection of flowers or foliage on to the surface. When you are happy with the arrangement, secure the pieces to the surface using a small amount of hot wax, or by rubbing the back of a very hot spoon over the candle surface where the flowers or leaves are to be attached. Push the pieces firmly in place.

2 Overdip the candles, following the instructions on page 60. When the candles are cold, use your finger to apply a small amount of gold rubbing paste to highlight the edges of the petals and leaves.

Making shell candles
1 Choose a selection of small shells that compliment each other in shape and colour. Using melted wax, fix them on to a plain white candle. Overdip the candle, following the instructions on page 60.

Making mosaic candles

1 Snip some mosaic tiles into tiny squares. Arrange the pieces on to a plain white candle, then fix using melted wax. Overdip the candle, following the instructions below.

Making chicken wire candles

1 Wearing heavy gloves, cut a piece of chicken wire large enough to wrap twice around a plain white candle. Wrap the wire tightly around the candle, twisting the ends together to hold it in place. Push the wire ends inwards, and where possible into the candle wax. Rubber bands will help to hold the wire secure, while you are twisting the ends together. Overdip the candle, following the instructions below.

Overdipping the candles

1 Place a quantity of paraffin wax in the dipping can. Any tall narrow metal container can be used. Stand the dipping can in a saucepan of water and heat until the wax reaches 93°C (200°F). The depth of melted wax that you need in the dipping can will depend on the length of your candle. Dip the candle into the hot wax for three seconds, remove and leave to cool. Trim the wick using scissors or a craft knife.

Making glass bead candles

1 Wash and dry an empty yogurt carton thoroughly. In a double boiler melt 100g (4oz) of stearin and a small amount of dye. Measure out 1kg (2lb) of paraffin wax and add to the double boiler, melt to a temperature of 93°C (200°F).

2 Prime the wick in the same way as for the plain white candles. Thread one end of the wick through the hole in a metal wick sustainer. Using pliers, crimp the tabs around the wick. Secure the wick sustainer to the centre bottom of the carton using blu-tack. Keep the wick upright and taut by wrapping it around a skewer or lolly stick, which is laid across the top of the carton.

3 Attach glass beads, flat side against the inside surface of the carton, using very tiny pieces of blu-tack.

4 When the wax has reached the correct temperature, remove the double boiler from the heat and pour the wax into the carton. Tap the sides of the carton gently to release any air bubbles trapped behind the glass beads. Adjust the wick so that it is straight and in the centre of the candle.

5 As the wax starts to set a conical shaped well will form around the wick. It will also shrink and a cavity will form below the surface of the wax. Pierce the skin with a needle to gain access to the cavity. If the wax is still liquid inside, leave it to set.

6 Reheat the remaining wax to 93°C (200°F). Top up the cavity with hot wax. Do not fill above the original wax level. Leave to harden for at least two hours, then remove the candle from the carton. Trim the wick to 1.25cm (½in) and remove any pieces of blu-tack stuck to the glass beads.

Making fruit candles

1 If you are unable to obtain dried orange or apple slices use fresh fruit, sliced and dried slowly in the oven.

2 Cut an orange juice or yogurt carton down to approximately 2.5cm (1in) above the height that you want the finished candle to be.

3 Prepare the carton in the same way as for the glass bead candle, and secure the wick

sustainer, with a primed wick attached, firmly to the bottom of the carton with blu-tack.

4 For the orange candle, melt wax, stearin and dye in the same way as for the glass beaded candle. For the apple candle, heat a quantity of white wax and stearin. When the wax has reached 93°C (200°F), remove the boiler from the heat and add a few drops of fruit essence. Pour the melted wax into the carton.

5 Leave the candle until the skin at the top is about 10mm (³/₈in) thick. Make a cut in the top of the candle with a craft knife and then carefully push an orange or apple slice down into the wax and up against the sides of the carton (see Candle Making Techniques, page 13).

6 Leave the wax until the skin is about 15-20mm (⁵/₈-³/₄in) thick, then cut away a square from the top of the candle and pour the liquid wax back into the double boiler. Allow the shell to harden, then refill with hot wax.

7 As the candle cools, top up with hot wax. Leave for two hours then remove from the carton and trim the wick to 10mm (³/₈in).

Making gravel candles

1 Wash and dry a large orange juice carton and cut to the finished size of the candle.

2 Prepare the wick and secure to the bottom of the carton in the same way as before. Melt 40g (1¹/₂oz) of stearin and 400g (15oz) of paraffin wax to a temperature of 93°C (200°F).

3 Tip 2cm (³/₄in) of gravel into the carton. Pour hot wax into the carton, just above the level of the gravel. Tap the side of the carton to release any trapped air bubbles. Leave the wax to firm up before adding more layers.

4 Continue adding layers of gravel and wax until you reach the top of the carton. Leave to harden for at least two hours. Peel off the carton and trim wick to 10mm (³/₈in).

Candle Troubleshooting

If you have made a candle that is less than perfect, re-melt the wax and pour again. But first, read on to find out how not to make the same mistakes twice

Moulded Candles

Fault	Cause	What to do
Candle has a pitted surface. Air bubbles in candle.	Wax too cold when poured. Poured too fast. Mould not tapped after pouring.	Check temperature before pouring. Pour slower. Tap mould after pouring.
Cracks in candle.	Candle too cold when topped up.	Top up sooner.
Candle is not smooth or has a thin layer of wax on the surface.	Candle too cold when topped up. Wax topped up above original candle level. Mould not completely clean.	Top up sooner. Take care to only top up to the original wax level. Wash in hot soapy water, or in the dishwasher.
Line around candle.	Mark left by level of water bath.	Make sure water bath is filled level with the top of the cooling candle.
Candle not a perfect shape.	Dirty mould. Cavity in centre of candle.	Clean thoroughly before reusing. Make holes in the top of the setting candle, then top up with wax.
Candle is stuck in mould.	Not enough stearin. Candle topped up too high.	Check recipe, and weigh ingredients. Top up level with the top of the candle. Put the mould in hot water or the fridge and try removing.
Candle will not come out of the rubber mould.	Mould may be damaged or have a hole.	Coat the outside with washing-up liquid and try again. Check inside the mould for damage before reusing.
Mould leaking from base.	Damaged mould, not enough mould seal used.	Seal with more mould seal, check mould for cracks.

Burning faults

Fault	Cause	What to do
Candle will not light.	Wick not primed. Mould seal or water on wick.	Hold candle upside-down to light. Clean off and dry wick.
Candle has small flame.	Impurities in wax. Wick too small.	Clean equipment and start again. Use larger wick.
Candle has large flame.	Wick too large.	Use smaller wick. Trim wick to 1-2cm ($1/2$-$3/4$).
Candle is smoking.	In a draught. Wick not burning well.	Move candle. Clean then trim wick or remake the candle using a different size.
Candle is dripping.	In a draught. Wax too soft. Wick not straight or too small.	Keep candles away from draughts. Check recipe. Use a larger wick.
Candle burns unevenly.	In a draught. Wick not central.	Move candle. Keep wick anchored while pouring wax
Candle not burning, pool of wax around the wick.	Wick too small or too short. Wick is not central in the mould.	Remake using a larger wick. Keep the wick central and straight when pouring the wax.

Wax Recipes

Rigid moulds

Shape	Height	Width/Dia	Wax	Additives
Cone	12.5cm (5in)	6.5cm (2½in)	165g (6½oz) paraffin	16g (½oz) stearin
Cylinder	9.5cm (3¾in)	6cm (2¼in)	200g (8oz) paraffin	20g (⅔oz) stearin
	10cm (4in)	6cm (2¼in)	200g (8oz) paraffin	20g (⅔oz) stearin
	11cm (4½in)	7.5cm (3in)	250g (10oz) paraffin	25g (1oz) stearin
	12cm (4¾in)	3.8cm (1½in)	115g (4½oz) paraffin	11g (½oz) stearin
	17.5cm (7in)	7cm (2¾in)	400g (15oz) paraffin	40g (1½oz) stearin
	20cm (8in)	5cm (2in)	225g (9oz) paraffin	25g (1oz) stearin
	22cm (8½in)	3cm (1¼in)	225g (9oz) paraffin	25g (1oz) stearin
Pyramid	16cm (6½in)	16cm (6½in)	1.4kg (2lb 14oz) paraffin	140g (5½oz) stearin
	22cm (8½in)	6cm (2¼in)	225g (9oz) paraffin	25g (1oz) stearin
Square carton	16cm (6½in)	6cm (2¼in)	500g (1lb) paraffin	50g (2oz) stearin

Alternative moulds

Shape	Height	Width/Dia	Wax	Additives
Flexible Mould	6.4cm (2½in)	4.5cm (1¾in)	80g (3oz) paraffin	8g (¼oz) stearin
Votives	4-8 medium tumblers		200g (8oz) paraffin	20g (⅔oz) microcrystalline soft
Floating	Several small press out moulds		280g (11oz) paraffin	25g (1oz) stearin
Floating	8 roses		500g (1lb) dip-and-carve	
Square Sand	7.5cm (3in)	7.5cm (3in)	475g (17oz) paraffin	48g (2oz) stearin

To find the correct quantity of wax needed for each mould. Fill the mould with water and measure: for each 150ml (¼ pint) of water use 100g (4oz) wax adding 10% stearin to increase the shrinkage. When making votives use ten parts wax to one part microcrystalline soft.

Acknowledgements

Thanks to David Constable at Candle Makers Supplies for his advice and loan of the candle making equipment needed for the projects; designers Jan Cox, John Underwood, Lynn Strange, Susan and Martin Penny for their imaginative ideas; and Jon Stone for his inspirational photography.

Suppliers

Candle Makers Supplies
28 Blythe Road,
London W14 OHA
Tel: 0171 602 4031/2
Shop and mail order for wax, moulds and equipment

The Candle Workshop
Lower Gelligroes, Pontllanfraith
Blackwood, Gwent NP2 2HY
Tel: 01495 222053
Shop and candle workshop

Index